What's the Next Move?

A U.S. Chess Masters Book

What's the Next Move?

A Book of Chess Tactics
for Children and Other Beginners

by **GEORGE FRANCIS KANE**
U.S. Senior Master

Charles Scribner's Sons • New York

To my brothers,

Patrick and Sean

Contents

Introduction

Chess is played the same way today that it was played in 1500. For nearly five hundred years people have been playing chess, from casual games in a park or coffeehouse to international tournaments which are followed with interest around the world. Chess attracts people from every country, of every social standing, and of all ages.

What is it that people find interesting in chess? The game itself presents challenging problems which are satisfying to solve. It has the competitive virtues of a sport and allows anyone to test his abilities against others. Chess helps to develop discipline, determination, and abstract reasoning.

The best way to discover why people enjoy chess is to play it yourself. Of course, you'll enjoy chess more if you win, and the player who wins is usually the one who sees more threats. Threat patterns come up frequently and mastering them will certainly improve your play. The positions in this book occur in actual games and are designed to train you to find common tactical devices. Each of the problems represents a critical point in a game, and you are challenged in each case to answer the question: "What's the next move?" Solutions are given in notation form on the back of each diagram.

There are several systems of recording chess moves. In this book a coordinate method called "algebraic notation" is used. In this system, each square is designated by a number and a letter, as shown in the following diagram.

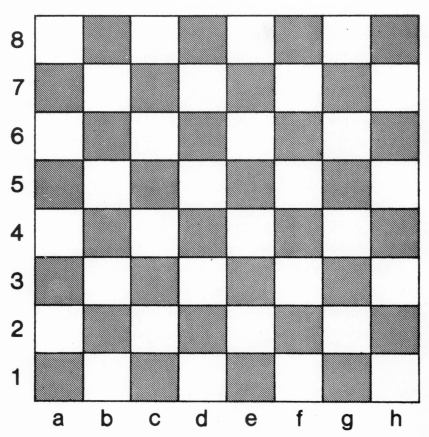

The squares are named by using first the letter, to designate the file, and then the number to indicate the rank. For example, the squares on the long black diagonal are named a1, b2, c3, d4, e5, f6, g7, and h8.

The pieces are identified by their diagrammatic symbol or by a capital letter according to the following code:

King	= K	Bishop	= B
Queen	= Q	Knight	= N
Rook	= R	Pawn	= P (optional)

In addition, the following symbols are used:

—	means "move to"
: or x	means "captures"
+ or † or ch	means "check"
++ or ‡ or mate	means "checkmate"
O—O	means "castling on the King's side"
O—O—O	means "castling on the Queen's side"

A move is recorded by indicating the piece moved, the square it starts from, then—or : as appropriate, and the square it moves to. Pawns need not be designated by 'P' and will not be in this book. Try to follow this short game in algebraic notation. The moves in the first column are White's, and in the second column, Black's. When Black's move is given without White's, it is indicated by three dots (. . .) preceding the move.

1. f2—f4	e7—e5
2. g2—g3	e5:f4
3. g3:f4	Qd8—h4‡

This is all that you need to know to read the solutions to the problems in this book. So, good luck—and happy solving!

GEORGE FRANCIS KANE

New York City, 1974

1

Tactics Not Involving Mate

The sixteen problems in this chapter involve tactics to win material rather than to force mate. The motifs required to solve these problems are explained below:

Fork: A fork is an attack on two pieces at once by a single piece. Problems 1 through 6 illustrate the Queen fork shown in the following diagram.

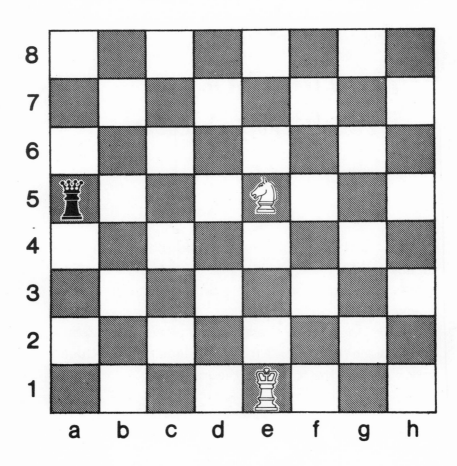

Black wins White's Knight.

Pin: A pinned piece is one which is attacked and cannot move because it is shielding a more valuable piece behind it. Problems 7, 8, and 12 illustrate the pin. In the next diagram White's Bishop pins Black's Queen to the King.

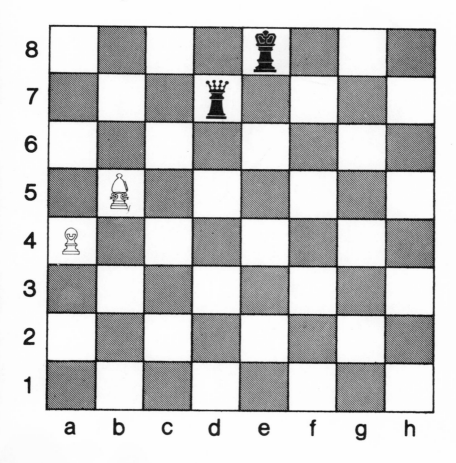

Discovered Attack: A discovered attack is really an uncovered attack in which a piece moves away to reveal an attack by a piece behind it. Problems 11, 13, 14, and 15 illustrate the discovered attack, as demonstrated in the following diagram.

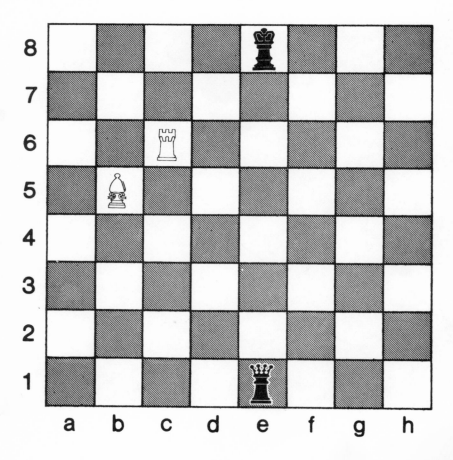

White plays 1. Rc6—c1+, discovered check, winning Black's Queen.

Skewer: A skewer, the reverse of a pin, is an attack on a piece which wins a less valuable piece behind it. It is also called an x-ray attack. Problem 16 illustrates a skewer, as shown in the following diagram.

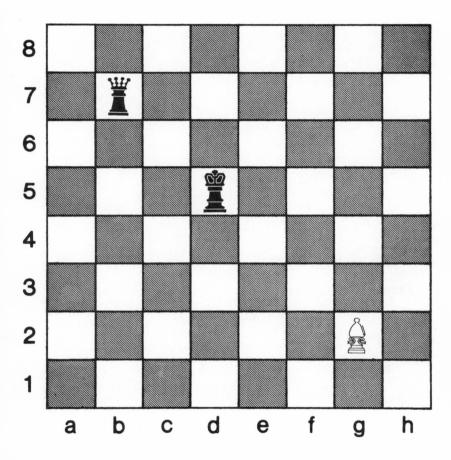

Removing the Defender: This motif is completely described by its name. An example is the following diagram. Further examples may be found in Problems 9 and 10.

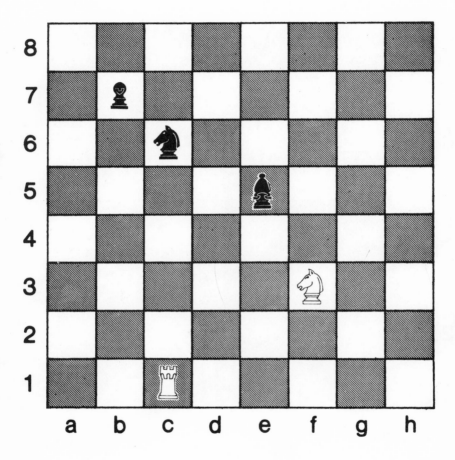

White wins material with 1. Rc1:c6, removing the defender of the Bishop, followed by 2. Nf3:e5.

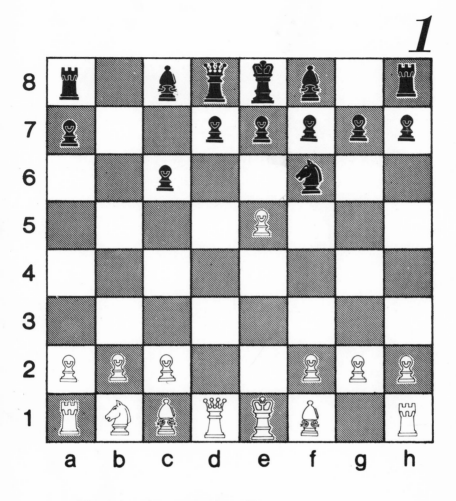

Black to play and win a Pawn.

(over)

1. . . .   Qd8—a5+

Black picks up the Pawn at e5 with this fork.

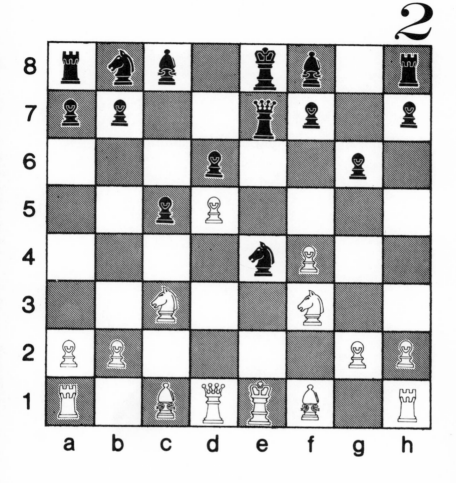

White to play and win a piece.

(over)

1. Qd1—a4 +

White forks the King and the Knight at e4.

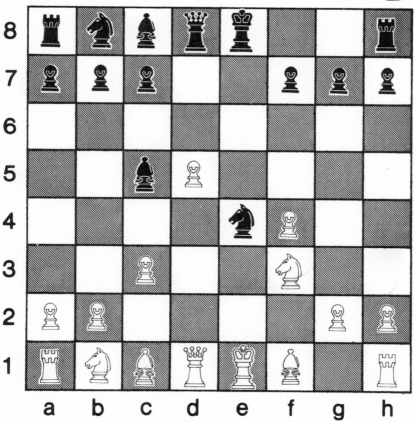

White to play and win a piece.

(*over*)

1. Qd1—a4 +

White forks the King and Knight.

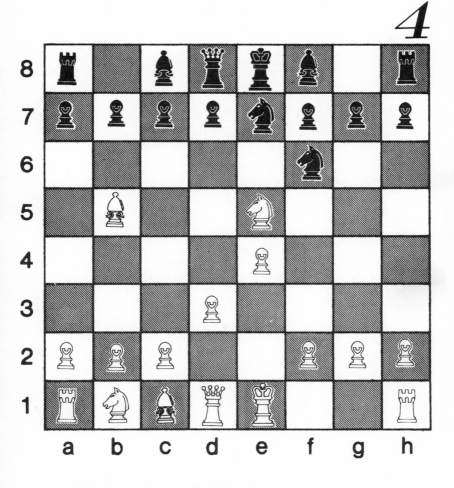

Black to play and win a piece.

(*over*)

Black can set up a Queen fork by opening the
a5—d8 diagonal with a gain of time.

1. . . .	c7—c6
2. Bb5—c4	Qd8—a5+
3. Any move	Qa5:e5

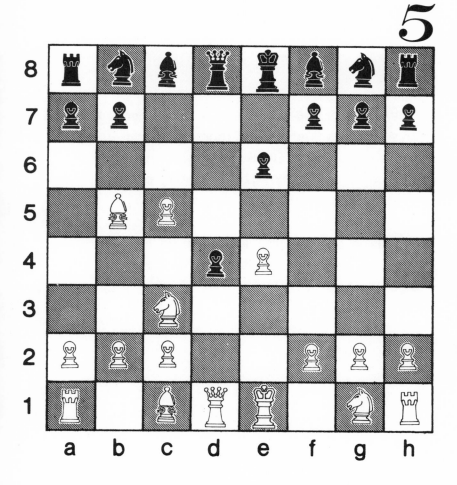

Black to play and win a piece.

(over)

With 1 . . . Ke8—e7 Black wins a piece. If White moves his attacked Knight, then 2 . . . Qd8—a5+ wins the Bishop on b5. If Black gets out of check with 1 . . . Nb8—c6 or 1 . . . Bc8—d7, White will capture it, with check, before moving his Knight.

This is a piece that Black would rather not win. After 1 . . . Ke8—e7; 2. Bc1—f4, d4:c3; 3. Bf4—d6+, White has a strong attack.

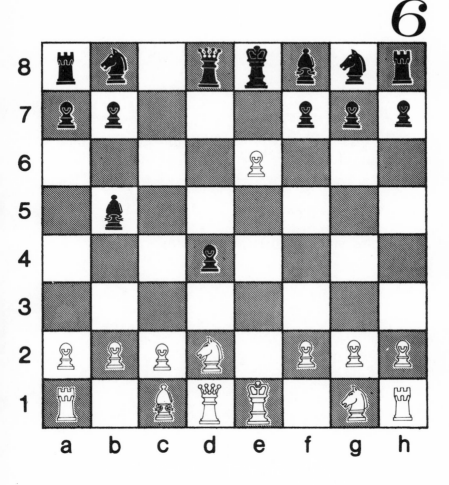

White to play and win a piece.

(*over*)

1. e6:f7+

This forks Black's King and Knight. The Pawn must be captured.

1. ...   Ke8:f7
2. Qd1—h5+

White wins the Bishop at b5 with a fork.

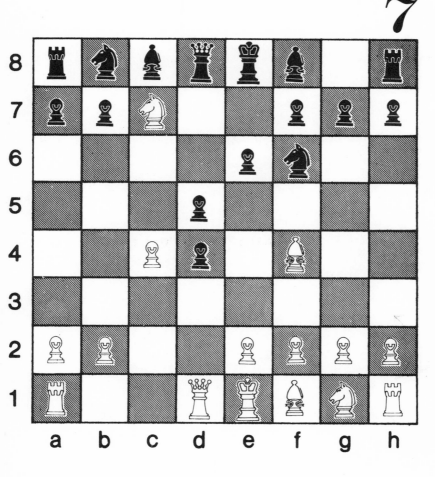

Black to play and avoid loss of material.

(*over*)

1. ...   Qd8:c7!

A temporary sacrifice.

2. Bf4:c7   Bf8—b4+
3. Qd1—d2   Bb4:d2+

Black is winning.

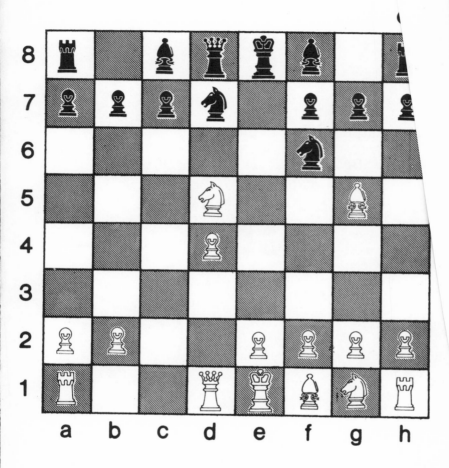

Black to play and win a piece.

(over)

| 1. . . . | Nf6:d5! |

A surprising way to break the pin.

2. Bg5:d8	Bf8—b4+
3. Qd1—d2 (forced)	Bb4:d2+
4. Ke1:d2	Ke8:d8

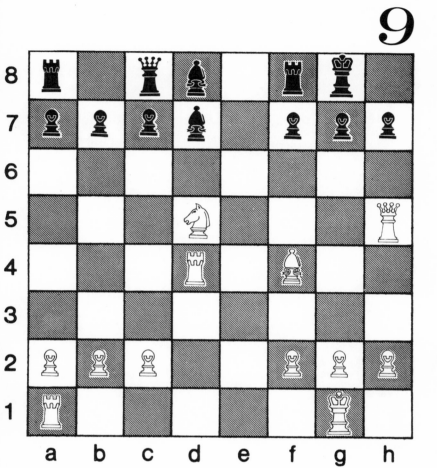

9

White to play and win a Pawn.

(*over*)

1. Bf4:c7! does it by the "removing the defender" motif. If now 1 . . . Bd8:c7; 2. Nd5—e7+ wins the Queen.

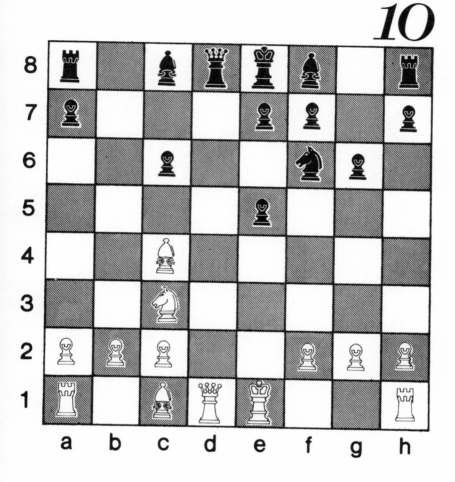

White to play and win Black's Queen.

(*over*)

1. Bc4:f7+ wins the Queen by removing the defender: 1 . . . Ke8:f7; 2. Qd1:d8.

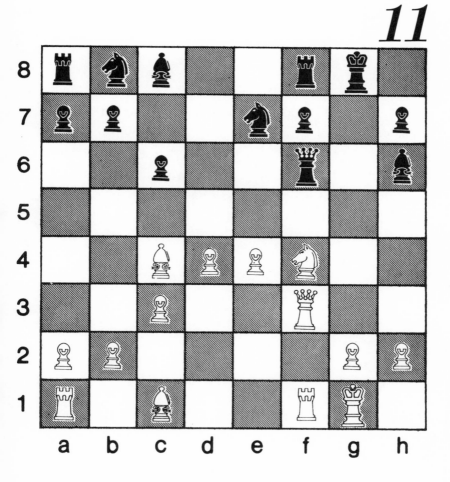

White to play and win material.

(*over*)

1. Nf4—d5! combines a discovered attack on Black's Queen with the theme of removing the defender of the Knight and Bishop. If now 1 ... Qf6:f3, 2. Nd5:e7+ followed by 3. Rf1:f3 wins a piece, or 1 ... Ne7:d5; 2. Qf3:f6, Nd5:f6; 3. Bc1:h6, when both the Knight at f6 and the Rook at f8 are under attack.

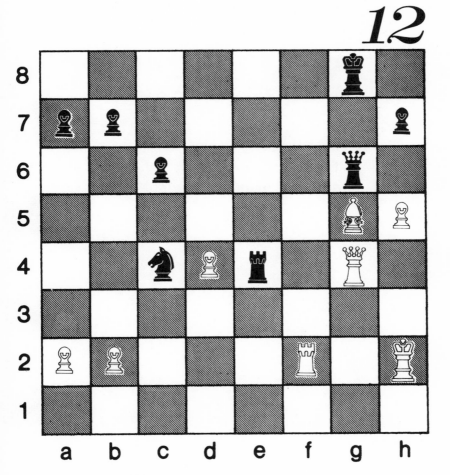

White to play and force mate.

(*over*)

1. Bg5—h6!

This pins Black's Queen and threatens 2. Rf2—f8++. Black can stop this only with 2 . . . Re4—e8, when 2. h5:g6 forces mate in a few more moves.

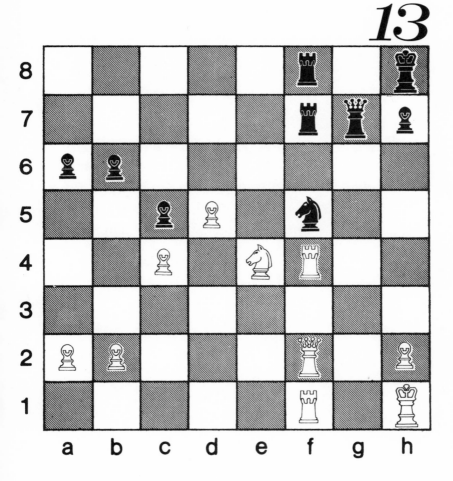

13

Black to play and win material.

(over)

1. ...   Nf5—d6!

This is a discovered attack on White's Rook. If 2. Ne4:d6, Rf7:f4 wins; or if 2. Rf4:f7, Rf8:f7, White's Queen cannot defend both the Knight and his Rook. White played 3. Ne4:d6, Rf7:f2; 4. Rf1:f2 and managed to draw in the Kane–Grefe game, U.S. Championship, 1973.

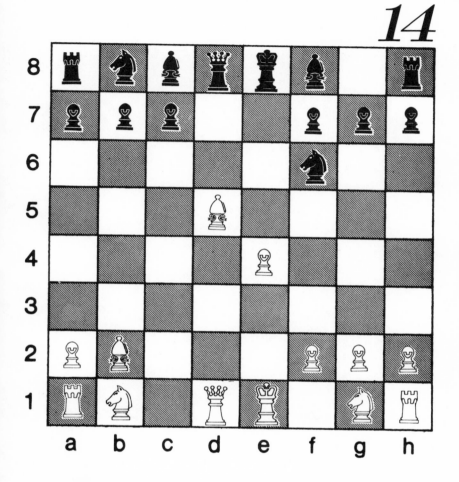

White to play and win Black's Queen.

(over)

1. Bd5:f7 + !   Ke8:f7
2. Qd1:d8

This is another instance of removing the defender.

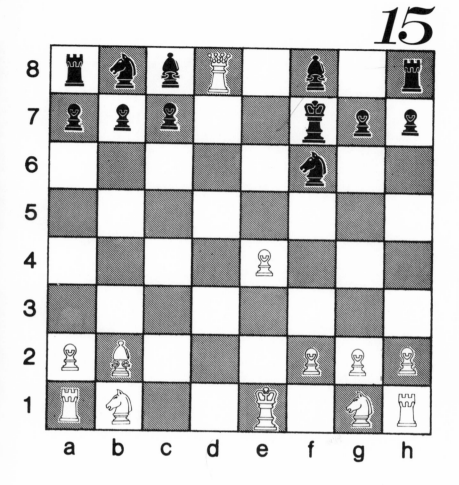

Black to play and win White's Queen.

(over)

1. ... Bf8—b4 + picks up the Queen with a discovered attack.

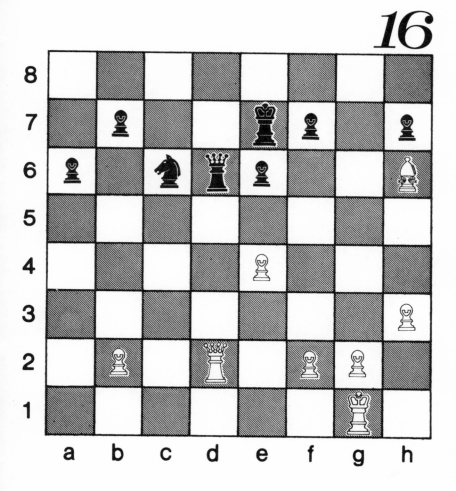

White to play and win Black's Queen.

1. Bh6—f8+! is a skewer, which removes Black's King from the defense of the Queen.

2

Tactics Involving Mate

The sixty-four problems in this chapter are arranged according to common mating patterns, as follows:

Study the patterns given before each section and try to utilize them when working out the solution.

Pattern A

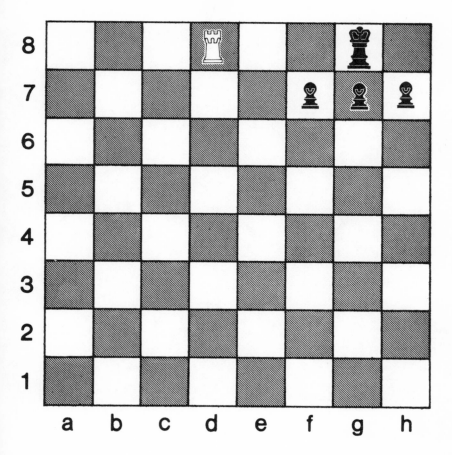

This is the "corridor mate" pattern in which Black's Pawns confine the King to the back rank.

Pattern B

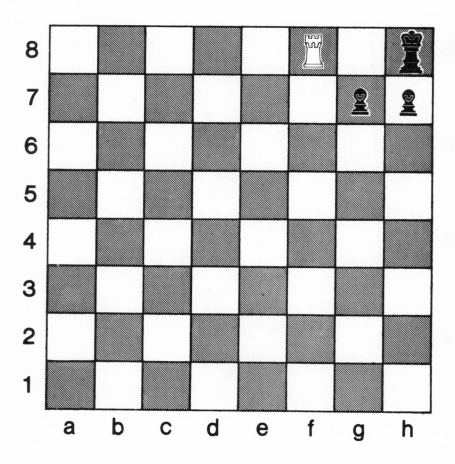

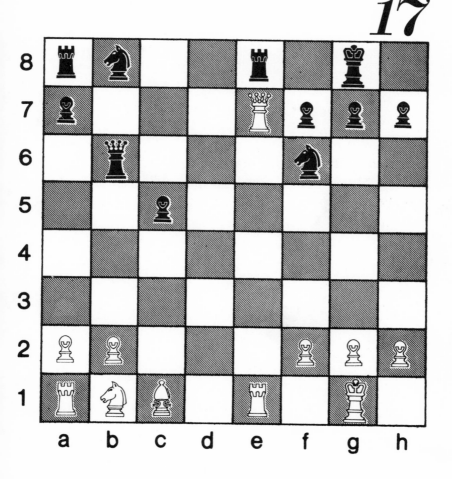

White to play and force mate in two moves.

(over)

1. Qe7:e8+ !   Nf6:e8
2. Re1:e8++

This is the corridor mate.

Note that if White's Queen had moved off the e file, Black would play 1 . . . Re8:e1++, another corridor mate.

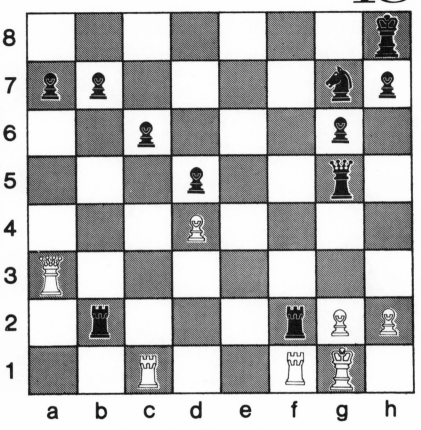

White to play and force mate in two moves.

(*over*)

1. Qa3—f8+   Rf2:f8
2. Rf1:f8++

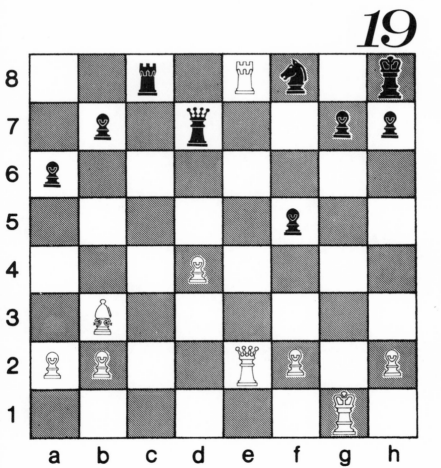

White to play and force mate in two moves.

(over)

1. Qe2—c4!

This threatens 2. Qc4—g8++.

1. ...   Rc8:c4
2. Re8:f8++

A corridor mate.

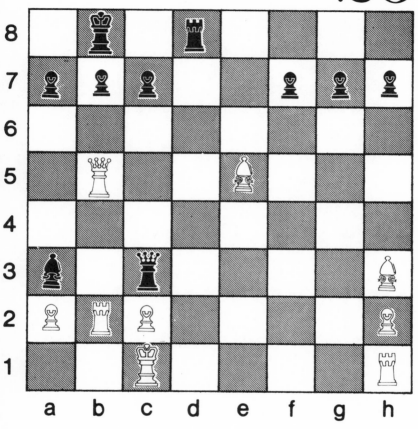

Black to play and force mate in three moves.

(over)

1. . . .   Qc3—d2+

First White's King is driven into the corridor.

   2. Kc1—b1   Qd2—d1+
   3. Rh1:d1   Rd8:d1++

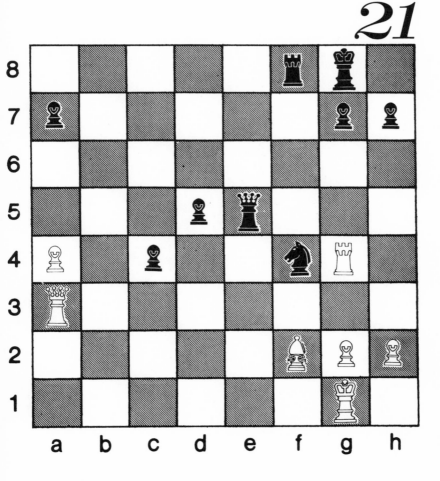

Black to play and force mate in three moves.

(over)

1. . . .   Qe5—e1 + !
2. Bf2:e1   Nf4—e2 +

This opens the f file and forces White's King into the corridor.

3. Kg1—h1   Rf8—f1 + +

1. Nd6—f7 +   Rf8:f7

If 1 . . . Kh8—g8; 2. Nf7:h6+, Kg8—h8; 3. Qc4—g8+ !, Rf8:g8; 4. Nh6—f7++ .

2. Qc4—c8+ !   Bd7:c8
3. Rc1:c8+   Rf7—f8
4. Rc8:f8++

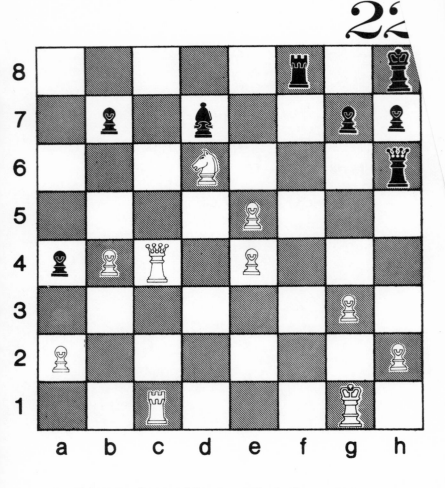

White to play and force mate in four moves.

(over)

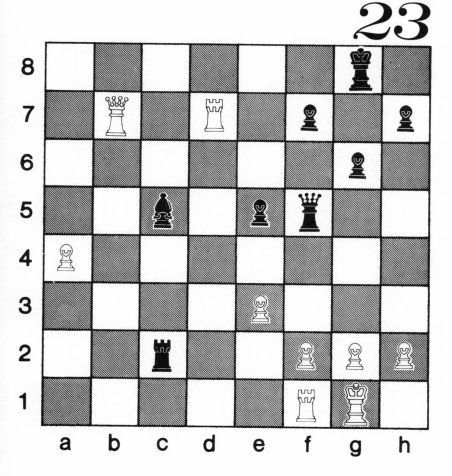

Black to play and force mate in four moves.

(*over*)

1. . . .   Qf5:f2+!
2. Rf1:f2   Rc2—c1+
3. Rf2—f1   Bc5:e3+
4. Kg1—h1   Rc1:f1++

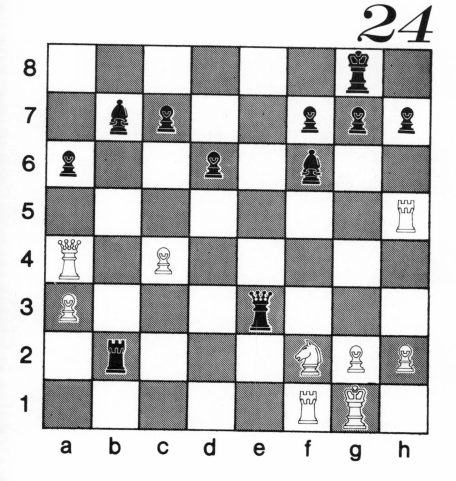

Black to play and force mate in five moves.

(over)

1. . . .	Qe3:f2+
2. Rf1:f2	Rb2—b1+
3. Qa4—d1	Rb1:d1+
4. Rf2—f1	Bf6—d4+
5. Kg1—h1	Rd1:f1++

In this section the corridor of Pattern A (page 41) is incomplete. In the first three mating positions (Patterns C, D, and E), a piece controls the square in the wall of the corridor not occupied by a Black Pawn. Pattern F is a case in which the checkmating piece covers the "hole in the wall."

Pattern C

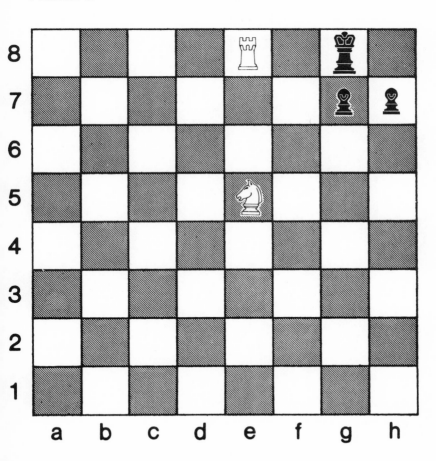

Pattern D

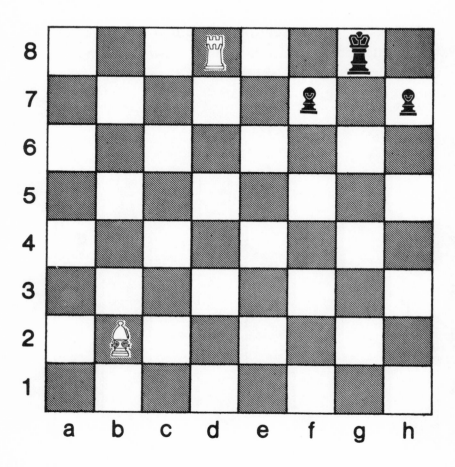

Pattern E

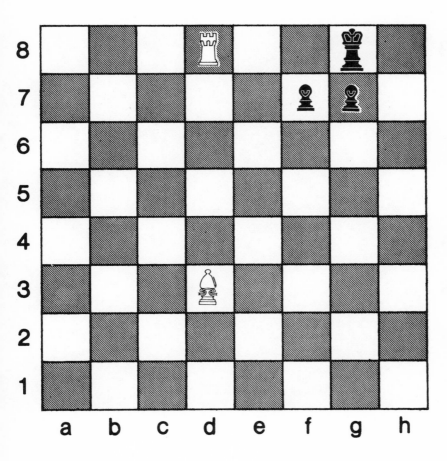

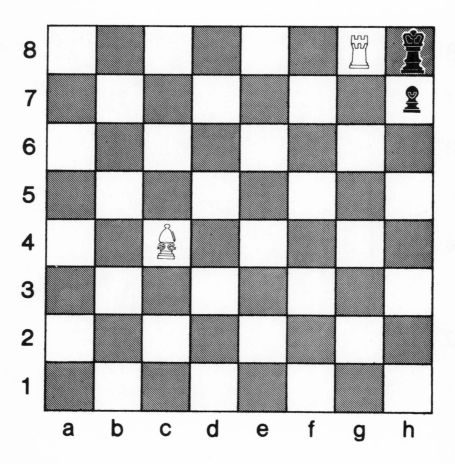

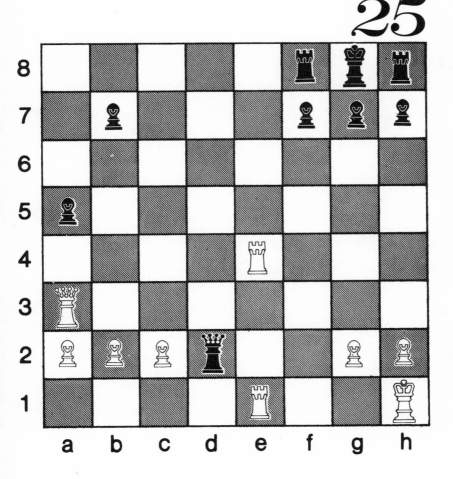

White to play and force mate in two moves.

(over)

1. Qa3:f8+!   Kg8:f8
2. Re4—e8++

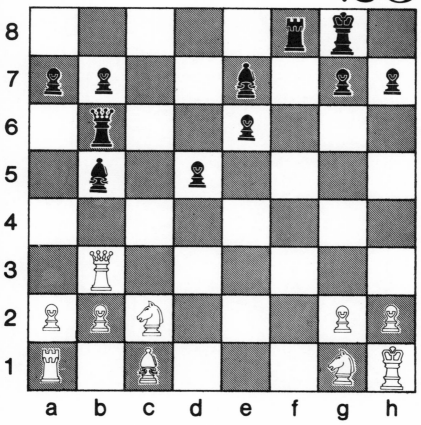

Black to play and mate in two moves.

(over)

1. . . .   Qb6:g1+
2. Kh1:g1   Rf8—f1++

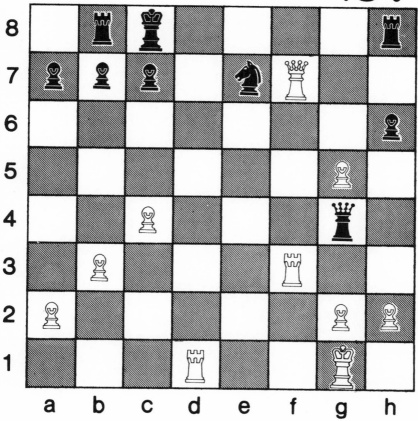

White to force checkmate in two moves.

(over)

1. Qf7—f8+   Rh8:f8
2. Rf3:f8++

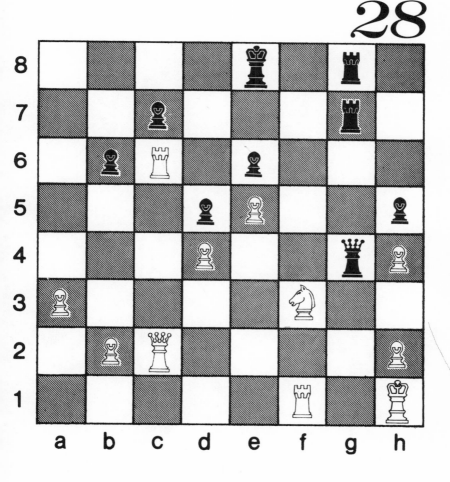

Black to play and force mate in two moves.

(over)

1. ...   Qg4:f3+!

This removes the defenders of g1.

2. Rf1:f3   Rg7—g1++

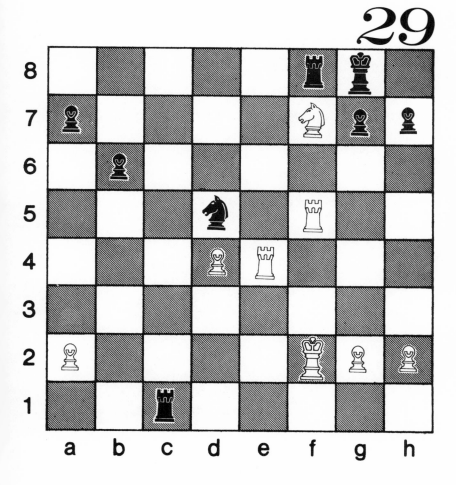

White to force checkmate in three moves.

(over)

The first stage is to force Black's King to h8.

1. Ne7—h6+ !   g7:h6
2. Re4—g4+   Kg8—h8

Now White has a back-rank mate.

3. Rf5:f8++

30

White to play and mate in three moves.

(over)

1. Qf2:f7+ !   Rf8:f7
2. Rc7—c8+   Rf7—f8
3. Rc8:f8++

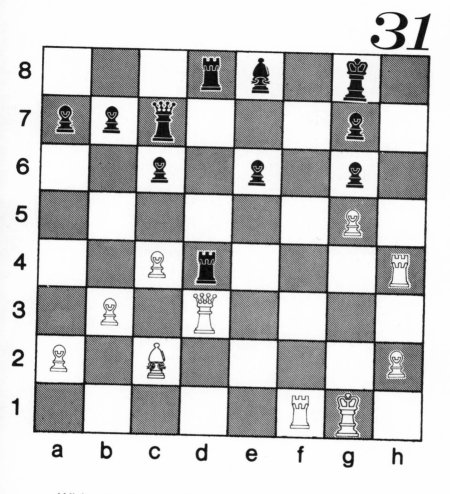

31

White to play and force mate in three moves.

(over)

1. Rh4—h8+!

This Rook sacrifice forces Black's King onto the open h file.

1. ...	Kg8:h8
2. Rf1—f8+	Kh8—h7
3. Qd3—h3++	

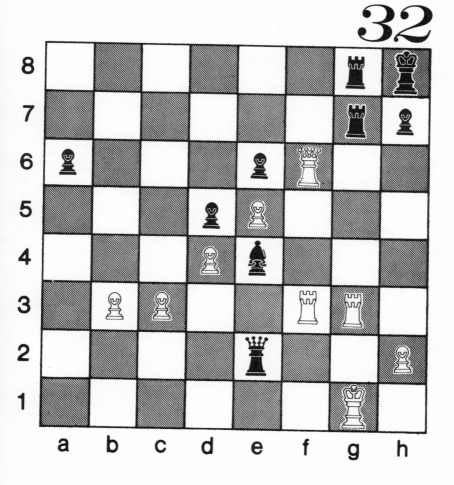

White to play and mate in three moves.

(*over*)

1. Qf6:g7 + !

Not 1. Rg3:g7, since Black recaptures with check.

1. . . .   Rg8:g7
2. Rf3—f8+   Rg7—g8
3. Rf8:g8+ +

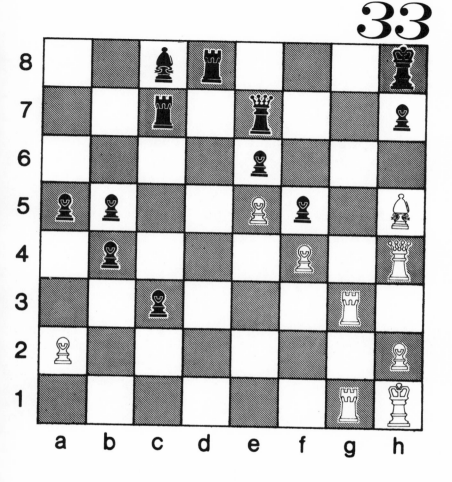

33

White to play and mate in three moves.

(over)

1. Bh5—f7!

This is a very difficult move to find. Black's Queen is pinned: if 1 . . . Qe7:f7, 2. Qh4:d8+ mates in the next move.

1.	. . .	Qe7:h4
2.	Rg3—g8+	Rd8:g8
3.	Rg1:g8++	

In some of the problems that follow, a new mating pattern is introduced—in which a Pawn two squares away from the opposing King controls two of its flight squares on the second rank. This is demonstrated below.

Pattern G

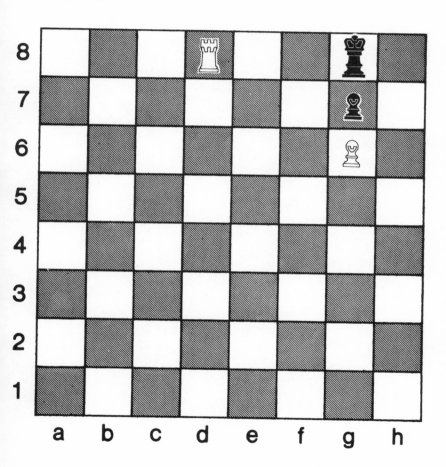

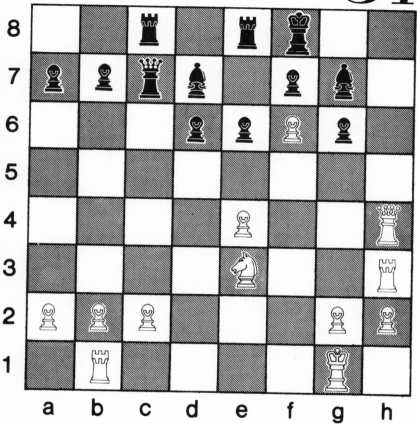

White to play and mate in two moves.

(over)

1. Qh4—h8+!   Bg7:h8
2. Rh3—h8++

It would be much harder to win if White played 1. f6:h7+ first.

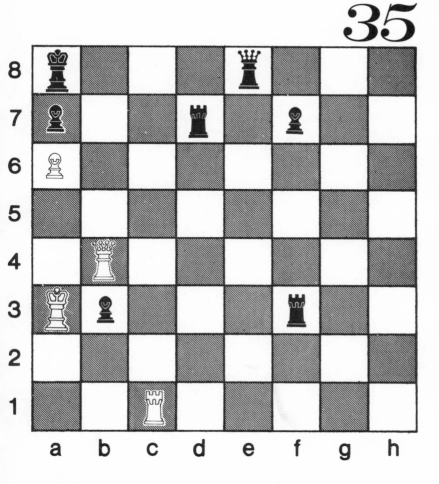

White to play and mate in three moves, at most.

(*over*)

85

If White could deflect Black's Queen, he would have Rc1—c8++.

    1. Qb4—e4+!

Now if 1 . . . Qe8:e4, 2. Rc1—c8++.

1. . . .	Rd7—d5
2. Qe4:e8+	Rd5—d8
3. Qe8:d8++	

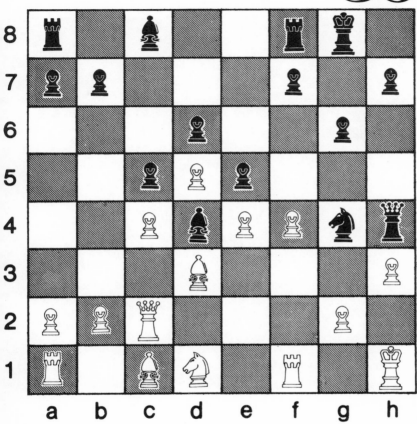

Black to play and force mate in two moves.

(over)

1. . . .   Qh4—g3

Now there is only one way to prevent 2 . . .
Qg3—h2++.

2. h3:g4   Qg3—h4++

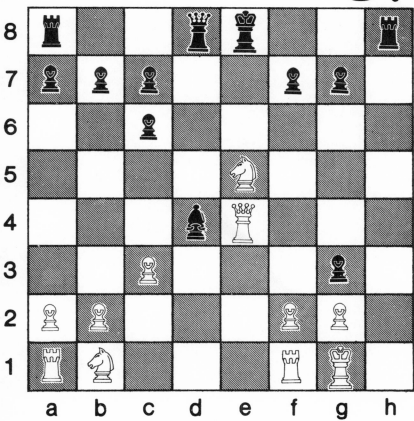

Black to play and force mate.

(over)

1.	. . .	Bd4:f2+!
2.	Rf1:f2	Qd8—d1+
3.	Qe4—e1	Qd1:e1+
4.	Rf2—f1	Rh8—h1+
5.	Kg1:h1	Qe1:f1++

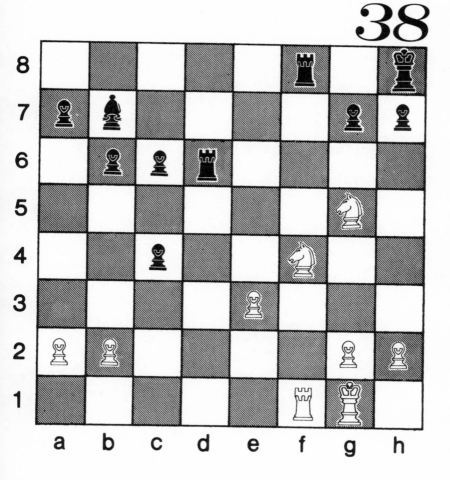

38

White to mate in two moves.

(over)

1. Nf4—g6+!

Regardless of Black's response, mate follows.

2. Rf1:f8++

39

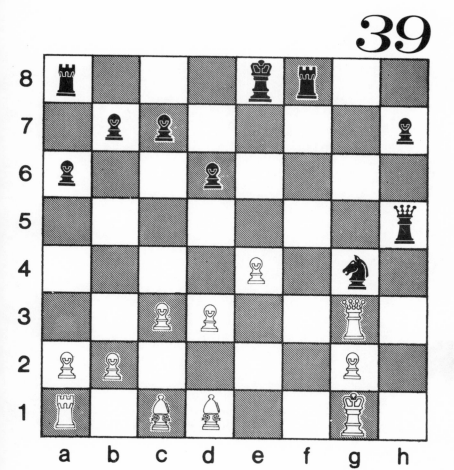

Black to play and mate in two moves.

(over)

1. . . .   Qh5—h1+
2. Kg1:h1   Rf8—f1++

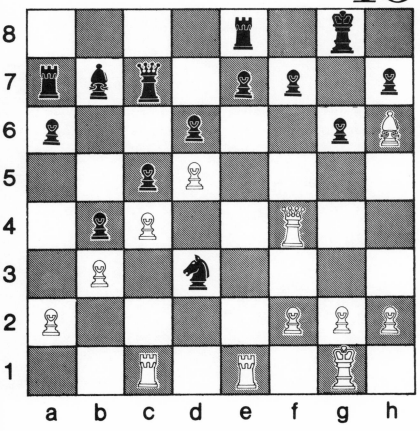

40

White to play and mate in two moves.

(over)

1. Qf4—f6!

This threatens 2. Qf6—g7++. The only defense is to capture the Queen, but the e Pawn is pinned.

1. . . .   e7:f6
2. Re1:e8++

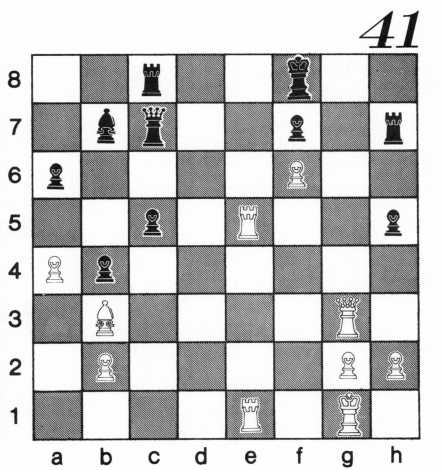

White to play and mate in three moves.

(over)

1. Qg3—g8+!   Kf8:g8
2. Re1—e8+   Rc8:e8
3. Re1:e8++

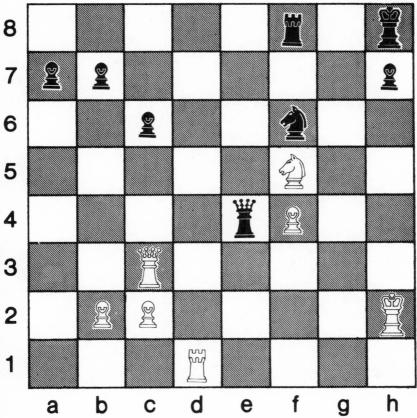

White to play and mate in three moves.

(over)

1. Qc3:f6+

This removes both defenders of the back rank.

1. . . .	Rf8:f6
2. Rd1—d8+	Rf6—f8
3. Rd8:f8++	

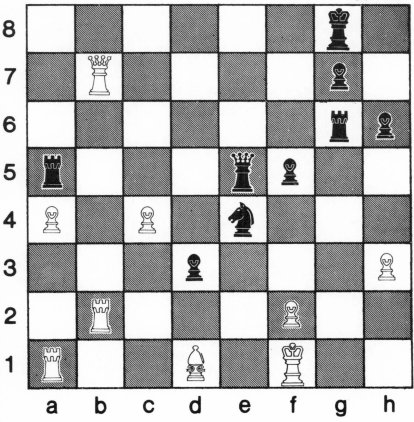

43

Black to play and mate in three moves.

(over)

1.	. . .	Ne4—d2+!
2.	Rb2:d2	Qe5—e1+!
3.	Kf1:e1	Rg6—g1++

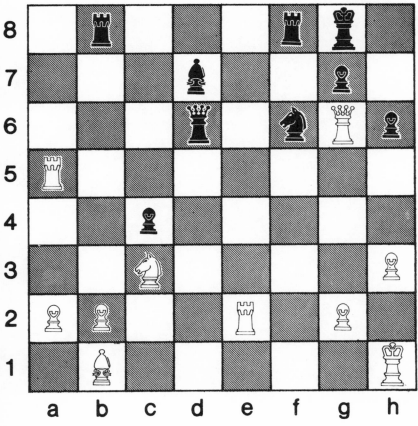

Black to play and force mate.

(*over*)

1. ...   Nf6—g4!

This move has two threats: 2 ... Qd6—h2++ and 2 ... Rf8—f1++. White cannot defend against both.

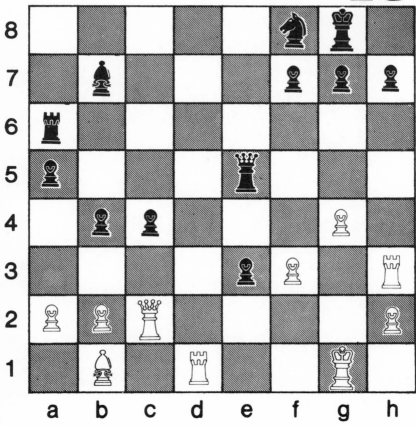

White to play and force mate in four moves.

(over)

1. Qc2:h7+!   Nf8:h7
2. Rd1—d8+   Nh7—f8
3. Bb1—h7+   Kg8—h8
4. Rd8:f8++

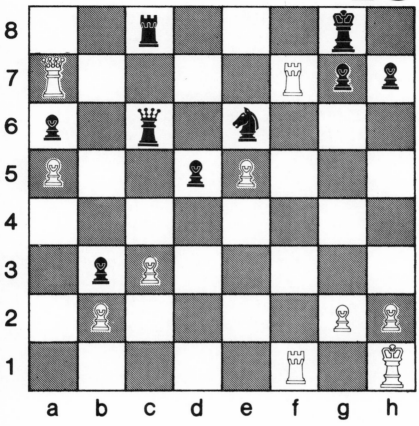

White to play and mate in four moves.

(over)

1. Rf7:g7+!   Ne6:g7
2. Qa7—f7+   Kg8—h8
3. Qf7—f8+! Rc8:f8
4. Rf1:f8++

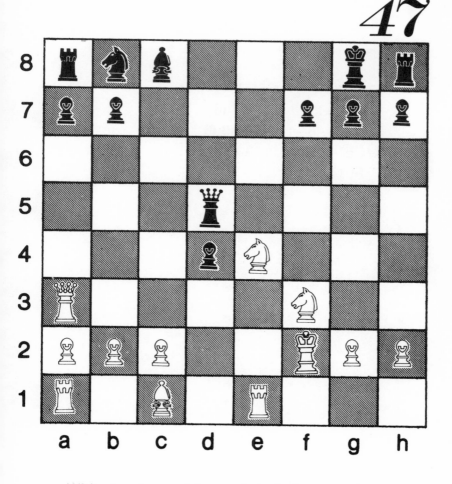

White to play and force mate in four moves.

(*over*)

1. Ne4—f6+!   g7:f6
2. Qa3—f8+!   Kg8:f8
3. Bc1—h6+   Kf8—g8
4. Re1—e8++

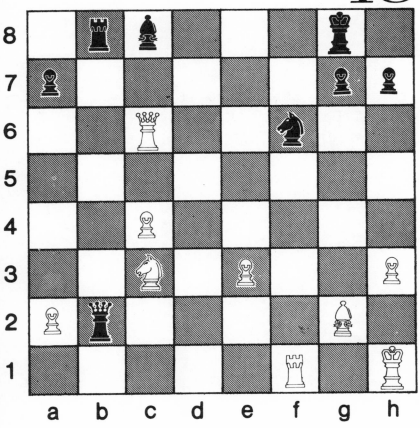

White to mate in four moves.

(over)

1. Qc6—e8+!   Nf6:e8
2. Bg2—d5+   Bc8—e6
3. Bd5:e6+   Kg8—h8
4. Rf1—f8++

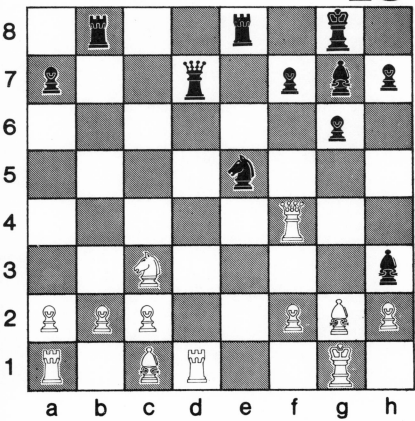

Black to play and mate in four moves.

(*over*)

1. ...   Qd7:d1 + !

This removes the defender of the back rank.

2. Nc3:d1   Ne5—f3+ !
3. Qf4:f3   Re8—e1+
4. Bg2—f1   Re1:f1 + +

In the next section, the mating pattern is as shown in the diagrams below—with the two Rooks checking on adjoining ranks or files.

Pattern H

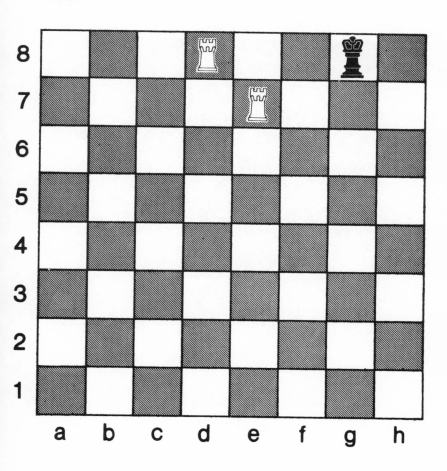

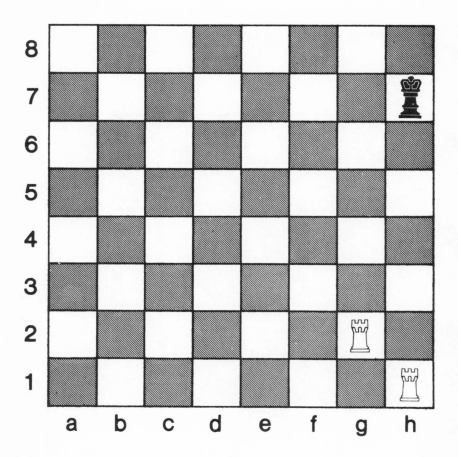

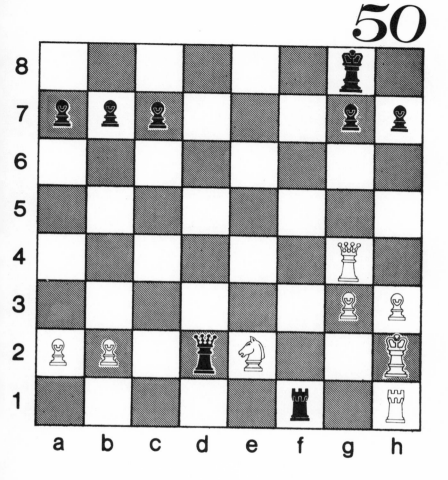

Black to play and force mate in two moves.

(over)

1. . . .   Rf1—f2+
2. Kh2—g1   Qd2—e1++

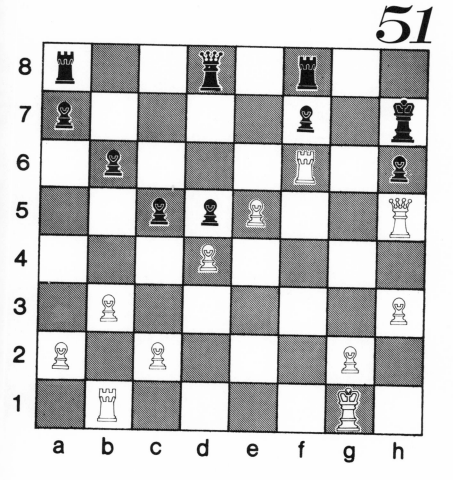

White to play and force mate in three moves.

(over)

1. Qh5:h6+   Kh7—g8
2. Qh6—g5+   Kg8—h7
3. Rf6—h6++

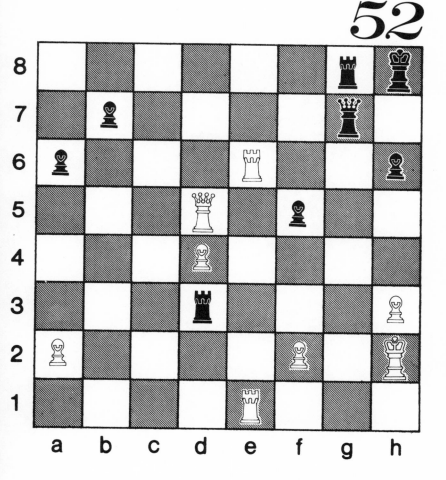

Black to play and force mate in three moves.

(over)

1. . . .   Rd3:h3 + !
2. Kh2:h3   Qg7—g4+
3. Kh3—h2   Qg4—h4+ +

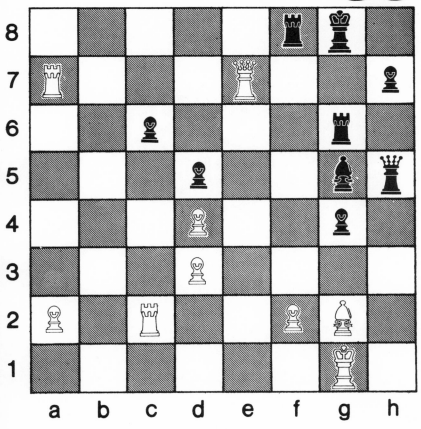

White to play and force mate in four moves.

(over)

1. Bg2:d5+!

This opens the c file for White's Rook.

1. ...	c6:d5
2. Qe7:f8+!	Kg8:f8
3. Rc2—c8+	Bg5—d8
4. Rc8:d8++	

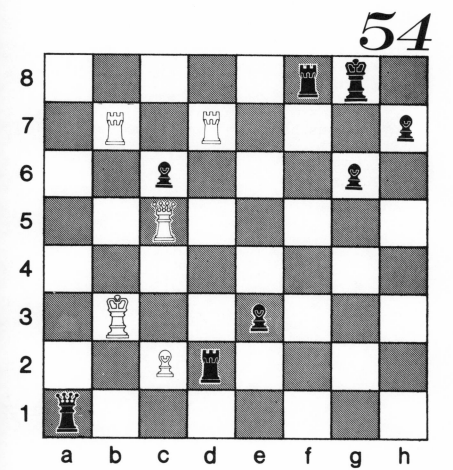

White to play and mate in two moves.

(*over*)

White clears the back rank with a Queen sacrifice.

1. Qc5:f8+ !   Kg8:f8
2. Rb7—b8++

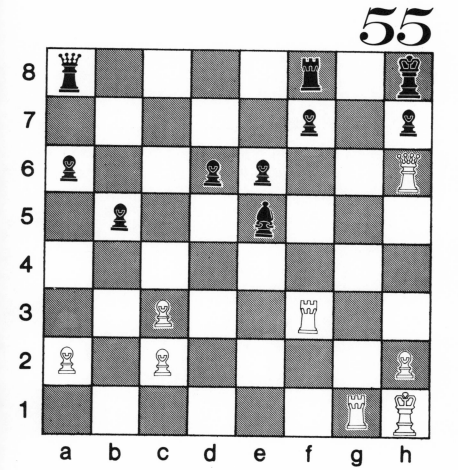

White to play and force mate.

(over)

1. Rg1—g2!

A quiet move which breaks the pin on the long diagonal. If now 1 . . . Qa8:f3, then 2. Qh6:f8++. Otherwise, there is no defense to 2. Qh6:h7+! and 3. Rf3—h3++.

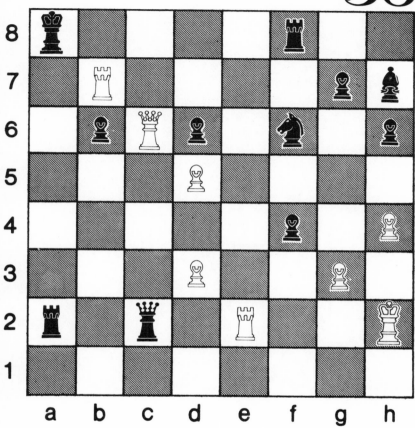

56

White to play and force mate in three moves.

(over)

1. Rb7:b6+   Qc2:c6
2. Re2:a2+   Qc6—a4
3. Ra2:a4++

In the next series the mating pattern is as in the diagram below—a corridor pattern tilted onto its side, with the square g7 controlled by White.

Pattern J

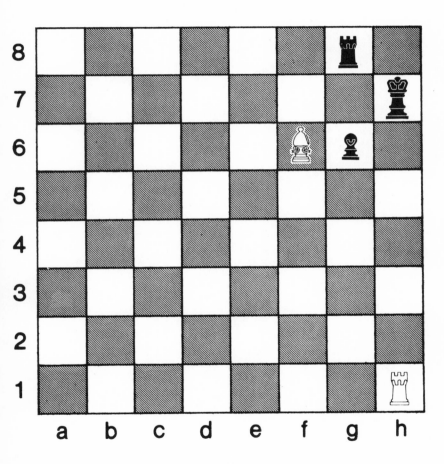

57

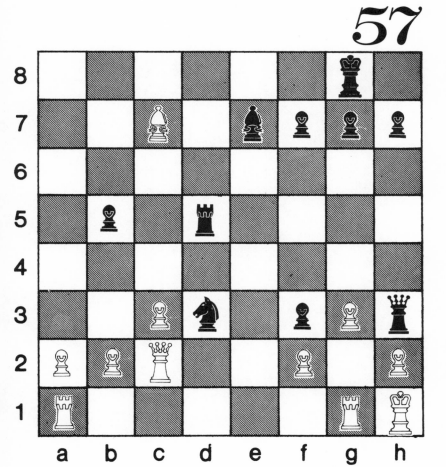

Black to play and force checkmate in two moves.

(*over*)

| 1. . . . | Qh3:h2+ |
| 2. Kh1:h2 | Rd5—h5++ |

This back-rank mate pattern on the h file occurs often.

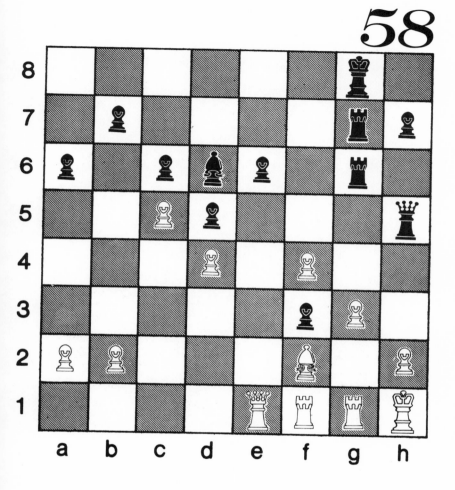

Black to play and mate in two moves.

(over)

```
1. . . .          Qh5:h2+
2. Kh1:h2     Rg6—h3++
```

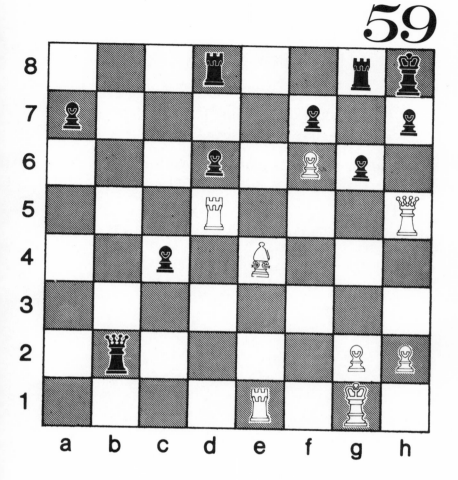

White to play and mate in two moves.

(over)

1. Qh5:h7+!   Kg8:h7
2. Rd5—h5++

The Pawn at g6 is pinned by White's Bishop.

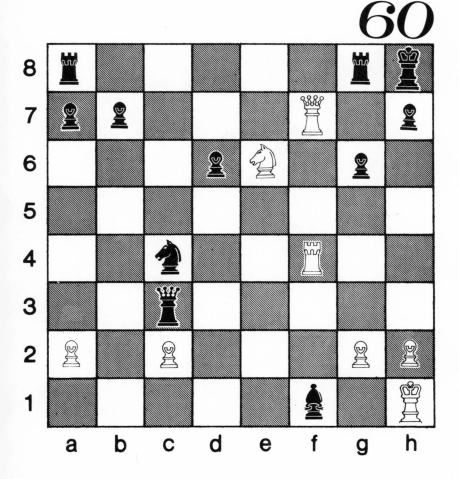

White to play and mate in two moves.

(over)

1. Qf7:h7+!   Kh8:h7
2. Rf4—h4++

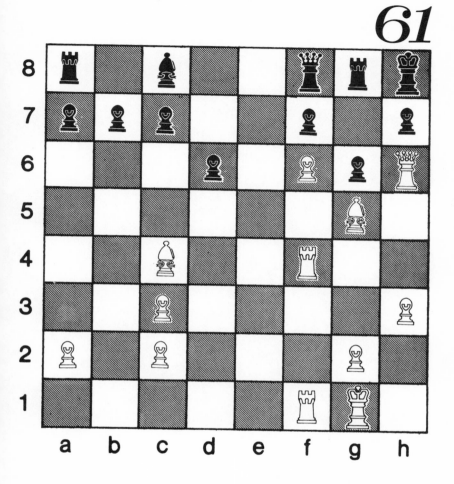

White to play and mate in three moves.

(over)

1. Qh6:h7+   Kh8:h7
2. Rf4—h4+   Qf8—h6
3. Rh4:h6++

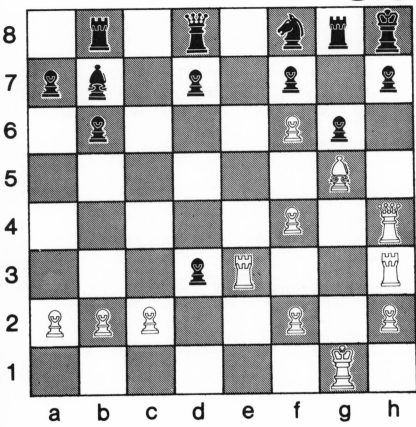

White to play and force mate in three moves.

(over)

1. Qh4:h7+!   Nf8:h7
2. Rh3:h7+!   Kh8:h7
3. Re3—h3++

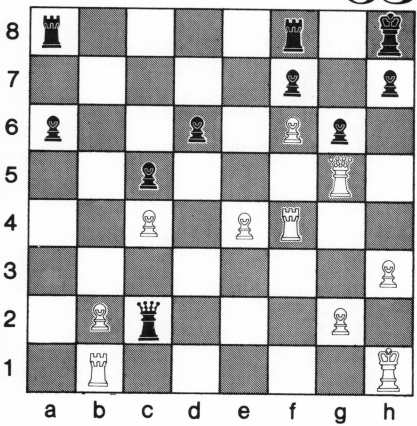

63

White to play and force mate.

(over)

1. Qg5—h6!   Qc2:b1+
2. Kh1—h2   Rf8—g8

Now White mates with 3. Qh6:h7+ and 4. Rf4—h4++, or with 3. Rf4—h4 first.

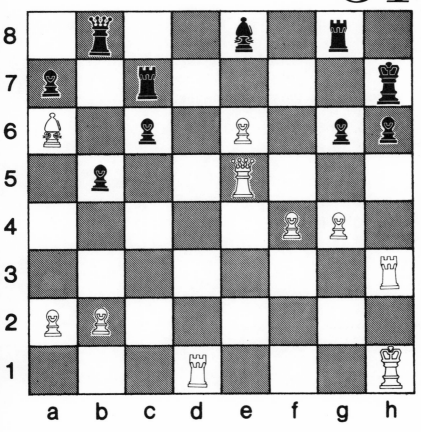

White to play and force checkmate.

(over)

This is one of the hardest exercises in this book, because White must make a quiet move.

    1. Rh3:h6+   Kh7:h6

    2. Kh1—g2!

Also 2. Rd1—d2 or d3 works. Black has no defense to 2. Rd1—h1++, since if 2 ... g6—g5; 3. Rd1—h1+, Kh6—g6; 4. f4—f5++.

Pattern K is similar to Pattern J except that the squares g8 and g6 must be controlled instead of g7.

Pattern K

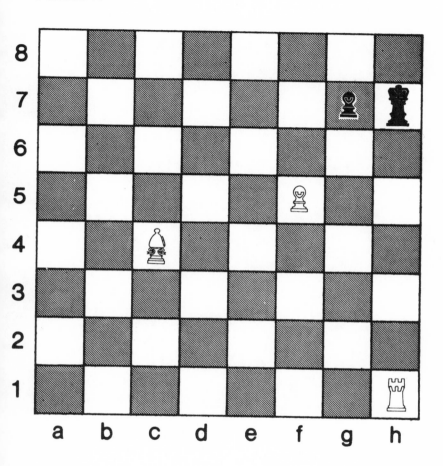

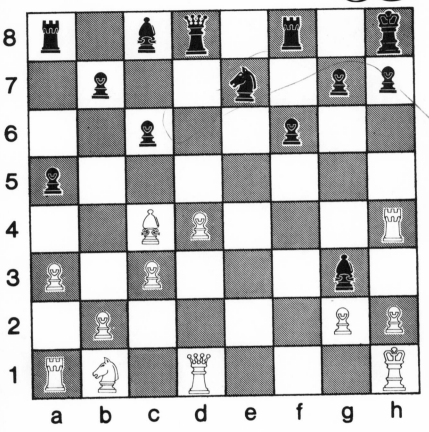

65

White to play and force checkmate in two moves.

(over)

1. Rh4:h7+   Kh8:h7
2. Qd1—h5++

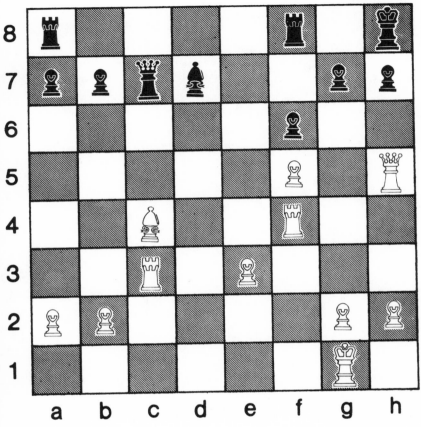

White to play and mate in two moves.

(over)

1. Qh5:h7+!   Kh8:h7
2. Rf4—h4++

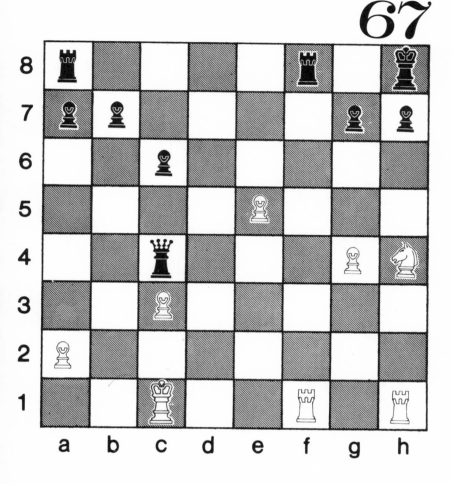

White to play and force checkmate in four moves.

(over)

Black is ahead in material, but White can keep him busy with a series of checks.

    1. Nh4—g6+   Kh8—g8

Forced; Black's h Pawn is pinned.

    2. Ng6—e7+   Kg8—h8
    3. Rh1:h7+ !   Kh8:h7
    4. Rf1—h1++

Pattern L continues the theme of controlling g6 and g8, but in a way that is characteristic of a combination called "Anastasia's mate," which is exemplified in the problems that follow.

Pattern L

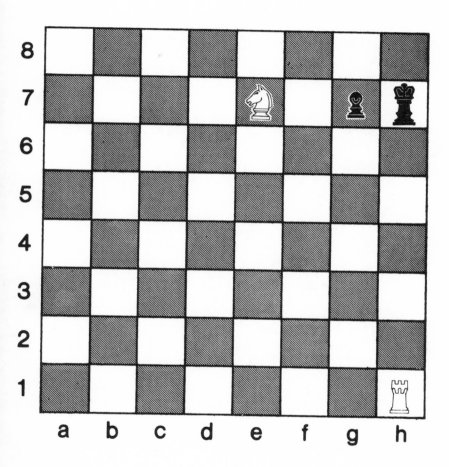

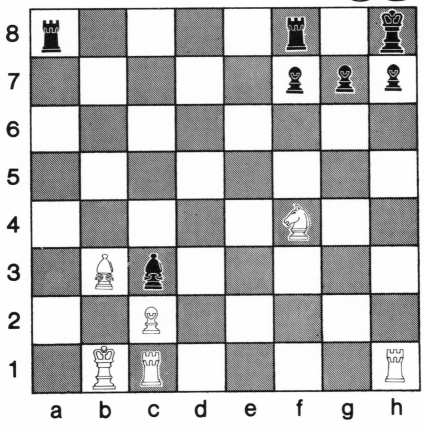

68

White to play and force mate in four moves, at most.

(*over*)

1. Nf4—g6+!

Now there are two variations:

1. ...	f7:g6
2. R:h7+!	Kh8:h7
3. Rc1—h1++	

and

1. ...	Kh8—g8
2. Ng6—e7+	Kg8—h8
3. Rh1:h7+!	Kh8:h7
4. Rc1—h1++	

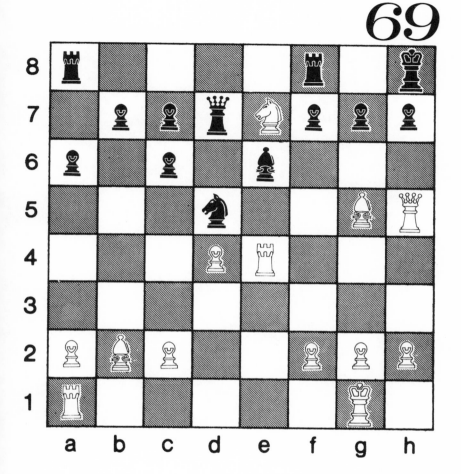

White to play and force checkmate in two moves.

(*over*)

1. Qh5:h7+   Kh8:h7
2. Re4—h4++

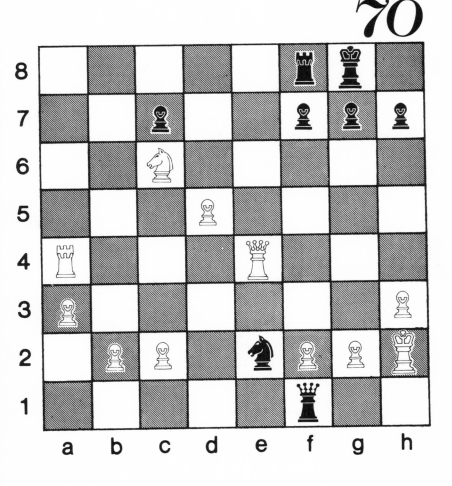

White to play and force checkmate in three moves.

(over)

1. Nc6—e7+   Kg8—h8
2. Qe4:h7+!   Kh8:h7
3. Ra4—h4++

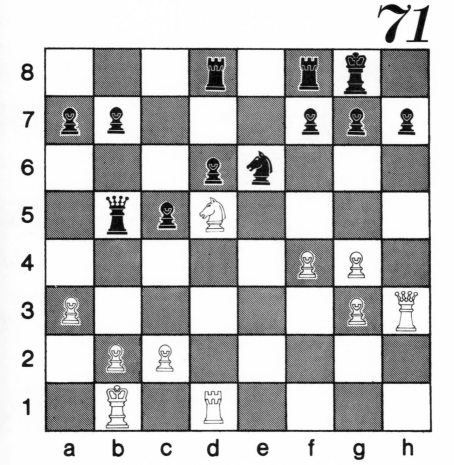

White to play and mate in three moves.

(*over*)

1. Nd5—e7+   Kg8—h8
2. Qh3:h7+!   Kh8:h7
3. Rd1—h1++

In the last group of tactical problems, the series of "sideways corridor mates" is completed. In patterns M and N, the g file is completely obstructed or else only the square g8 must be controlled by White.

Pattern M

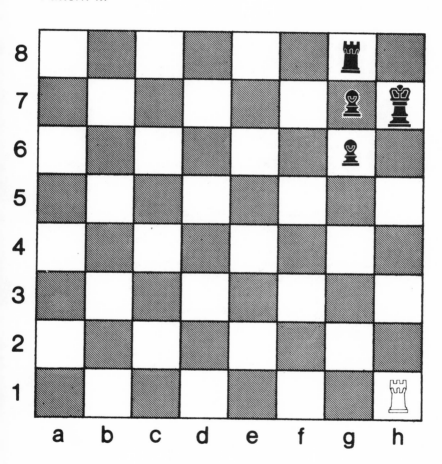

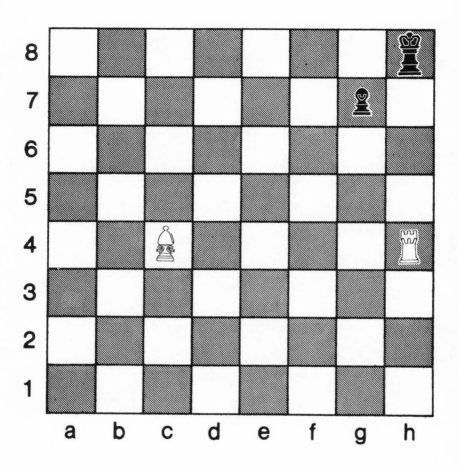

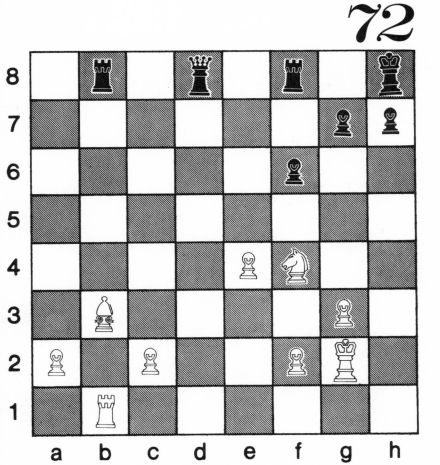

White to play and mate in two moves.

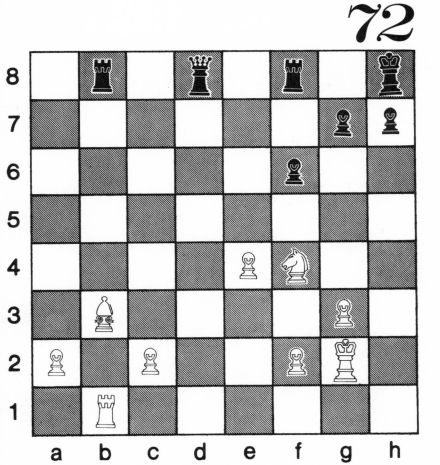

(over)

1. Nf4—g6+!   h7:g6
2. Rb1—h1++

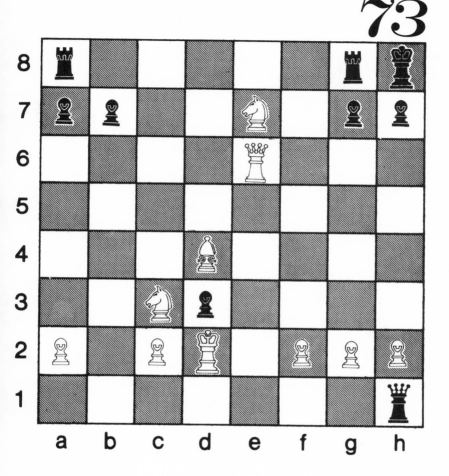

White to play and mate in two moves.

(over)

1. Ne7—g6+   h7:g6
2. Qe6—h3++

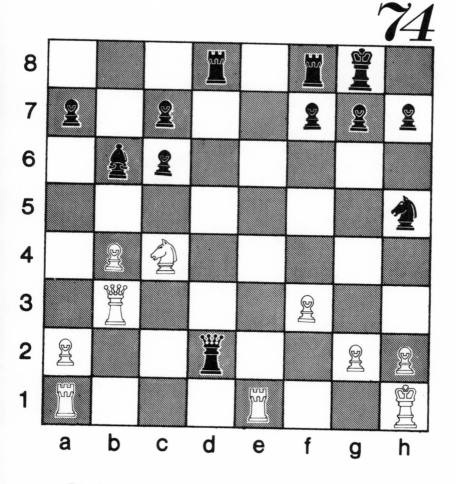

Black to play and force checkmate in two moves.

(over)

1. . . .	Nh5—g3+
2. h2:g3	Qd2—h6++

Black's Bishop at b6 controls the g1 square.

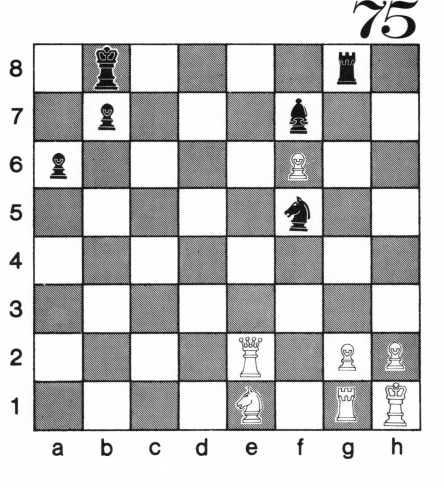

Black to play and mate in three moves.

(*over*)

Black must clear the h file for a corridor mate.

1.	. . .	Nf5—g3+!
2.	h2:g3	Rg8—h8+
3.	Qe2—h5	Rh8:h5++

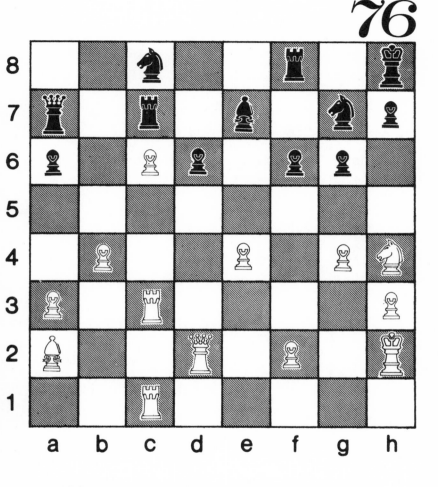

76

White to play and force mate in two moves.

(*over*)

1. Nh4:g6+!   h7:g6
2. Qd2—h6++

The Bishop on a2 controls g8.

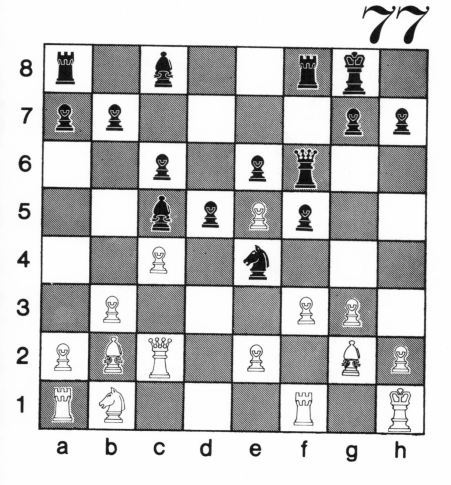

Black to play and mate in three moves.

(over)

1. ...   Ne4:g3+!
2. h2:g3   Qf6—h6+
3. Bg2—h3   Qh6:h3++

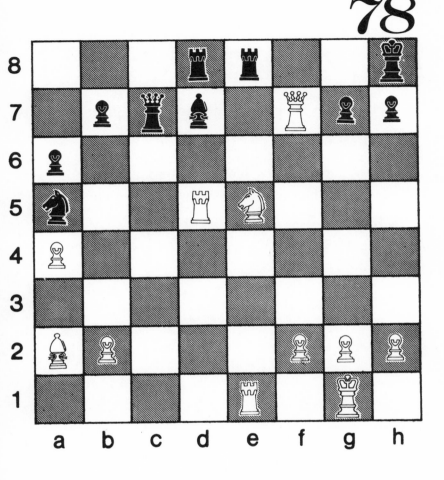

78

White to play and checkmate in three moves.

(*over*)

First the h file must be opened with a sacrifice.

    1. Ne5—g6+!   h7:g6

Now, since Black is threatening 2 ... Re8:1++, White must bring his Queen to the h file with a series of checks.

    2. Rd5—h5+!   g6:h5
    3. Qf7—h5++

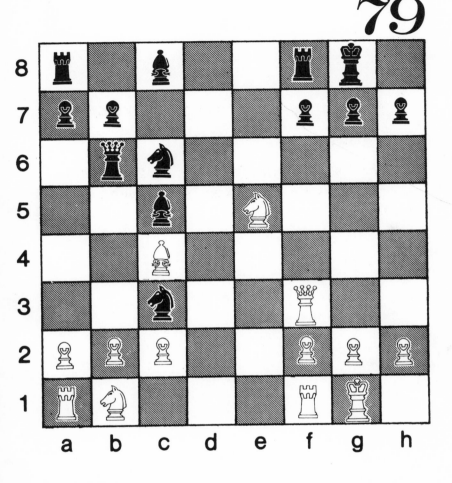

79

White to play and force mate in three moves.

(over)

1. Bc4:f7+

Now there are two variations:

1. ...	Kg8—h8
2. Ne5—g6+!	h7:g6
3. Qf3—h3++	

and

1. ...	Rf8:f7
2. Qf3:f7+	Kg8—h8
3. Qf7—f8++	

A corridor mate.

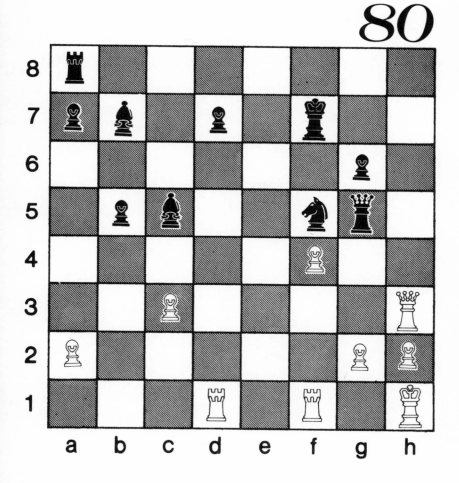

Black to play and force mate in three moves.

(over)

Black must get White's Queen and h Pawn off the file.

1. . . .	Qg5:g2+!!
2. Qh3:g2	Nf5—g3+!
3. h2:g3	Ra8—h8++

3

The Endgame

The nine problems in this chapter deal with the endgame. In the endgame the most important goal is to promote a Pawn. The Pawn which is the candidate for promotion is the *passed Pawn*. A passed Pawn is one that is not obstructed by an enemy Pawn on the same file or an adjoining one. In the following diagram, White's c Pawn and Black's a Pawn are passed, while on the other wing neither Pawn is passed.

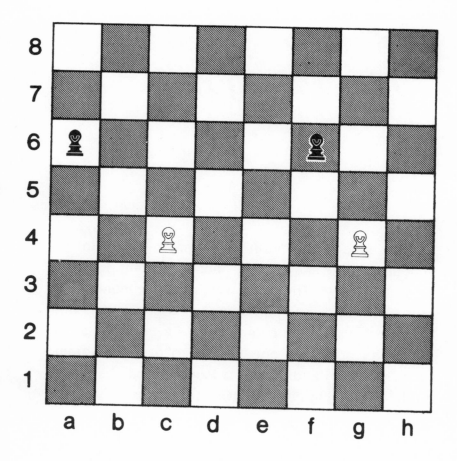

The first law of passed Pawns is the *square of the
Pawn*. To determine if the opponent's King is close
enough to stop a Pawn from promoting, draw a diagonal line from the Pawn to the eighth rank. That line is
the diagonal of the square of the Pawn. If the opponent's King is inside this square or, to move, can enter

it, it can catch the Pawn. If the opponent's King is not inside the square, the Pawn will promote.

The Square of the Pawn

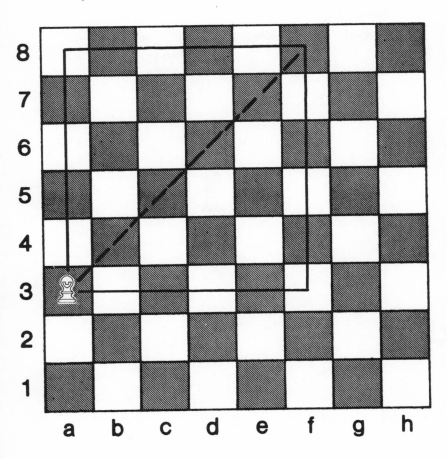

If the defender's King is inside the square of the Pawn, then it must be supported to be promoted. With a King and Pawn vs. a King, the superior side's King must be in front of the Pawn to escort it in. In order to accomplish this, the *opposition* is an important tool. The term describes the relationship between two Kings that are facing each other, one square apart on a rank or file, as in the next diagram.

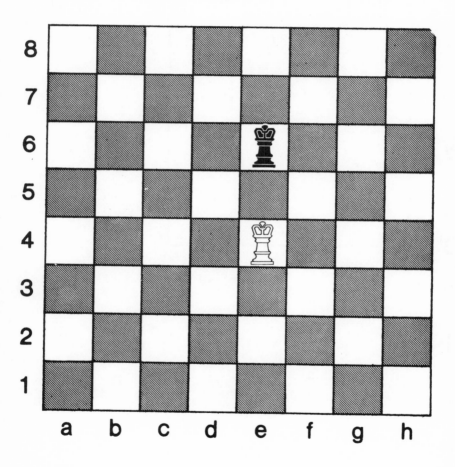

Neither side, to move, can advance with his King. However, if White is to move, he must step aside and let Black's King advance. The player who has the opposition is the player whose opponent is to move.

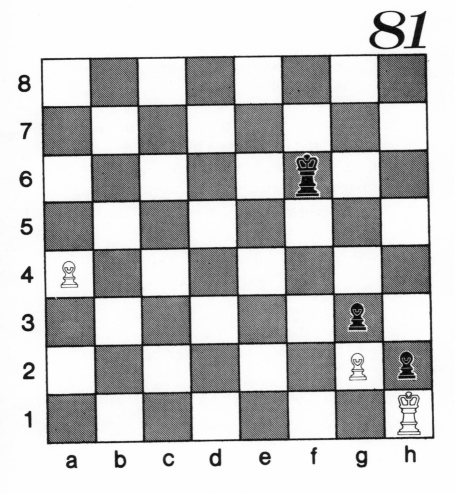

Can Black draw?

(over)

Black to play can draw because he can step inside the square of the passed Pawn by 1 ... Kf6—e6. When he captures the Pawn, White will be stalemated. With White to move, Black's King is too far away from White's a Pawn to stop it.

White to play and win.

(over)

White's King must get in front of his Pawn to control the squares in its path.

1.	Kd4—c5	Kc6—d7
2.	Kc5—b6	Kd7—c8
3.	Kb6—c6	Kc8—d8
4.	Kc6—b7	Kd8—d7
5.	c4—c5	

White's Pawn promotes in three more moves.

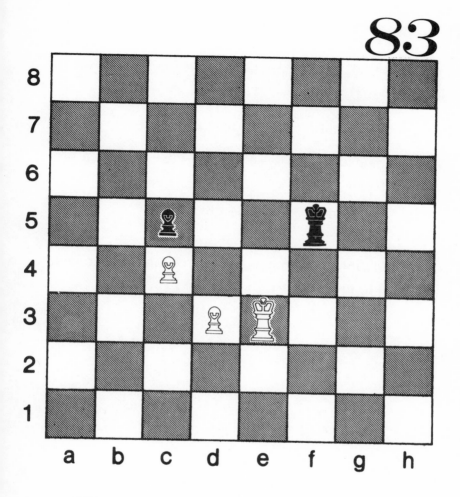

83

White to play and win.

(over)

1. d3—d4   c5:d4+

If instead 1 . . . Kf5—e6, 2. d4—d5+ creates a protected passed Pawn.

2. Ke3:d4   Kf5—e6
3. Kd4—c5

And White's King gets in front of the Pawn to clear its path to promotion.

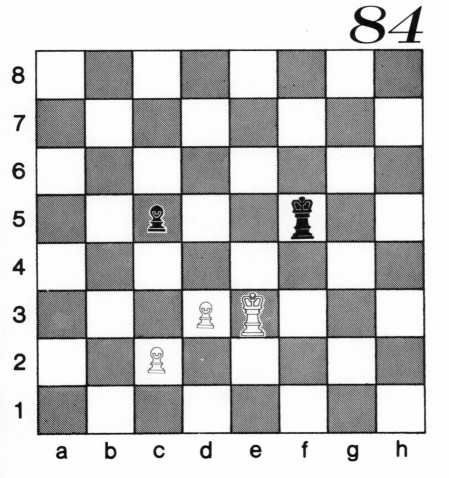

White to play and win.

(over)

1.	c2—c3	Kf5—e5
2.	c3—c4	Ke5—f5
3.	d3—d4	`

Thus we reach the previous example.

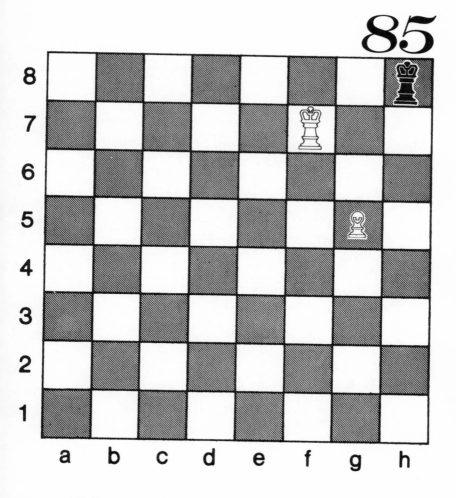

White to play and win.

(over)

A mistake would be 1. g5—g6? stalemate. White
must squeeze Black's King out of the corner.

1.	Kf7—g6	Kh8—g8
2.	Kg6—h6	Kg8—h8
3.	g5—g6	Kh8—g8
4.	g6—g7	Kg8—f7
5.	Kh6—h7	

The Pawn promotes.

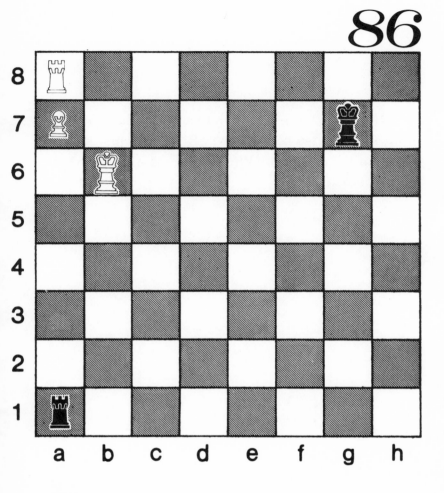

Black to play and draw.

(over)

After 1 . . . Ra1—b1+, White's King must move away from the defense of his Pawn. Black will just keep his Rook on the a file until White's King is at b6 or b7, and then check it away.

Black to play and draw.

(over)

With 1 . . . Kf6—g7!, Black prevents a Rook check which would allow the Pawn to Queen. Now if White tries to support the Pawn with his King, it will be checked away from behind.

If Black had played instead 1 . . . Kf6—f7: 2. Ra8—h8, Ra1:a7; 3. Rh8—h7+ wins the Rook with an x-ray attack.

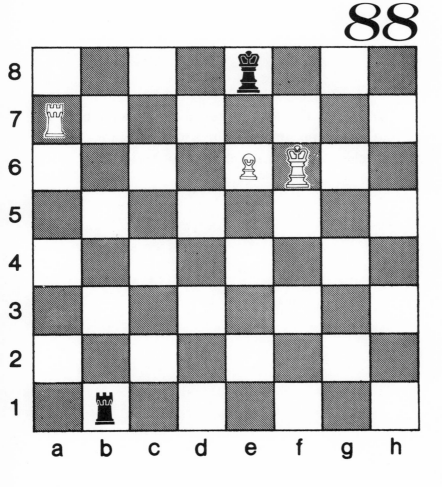

88

Black to play and draw.

(*over*)

With 1 . . . Rb1—f1+ a series of checks begins that White cannot escape. If White's King runs for cover on a8, Black's Rook will win the White Pawn.

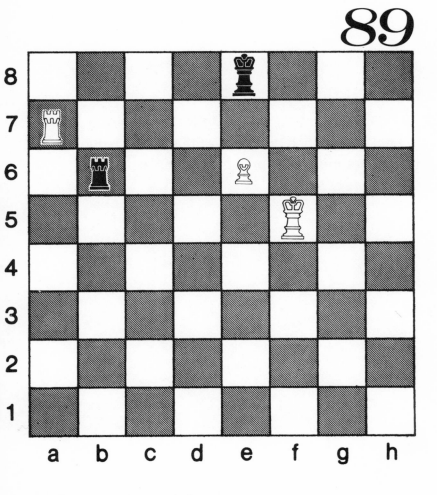

Black to play and draw.

(over)

By playing 1 . . . Rb6—b1 Black threatens a series of checks from behind that White's King cannot avoid. Compare this to the previous example.

ABOUT THE AUTHOR

GEORGE FRANCIS KANE is one of the United States' most promising young Chess Masters. Holding the title U.S. Senior Master, he represented the United States in the 1972 Olympics, competed in the 1973 U.S. Championship, and is past champion of the Marshall Chess Club in New York.

He is vice president of U.S. Chess Masters, Inc., and is active as a chess teacher, writer, and lecturer. He is currently teaching at the New School for Social Research and The Herbert H. Lehman College in New York, in addition to running a large chess program for elementary school children at the Creative Arts Workshop in Port Washington, New York.

He was born in California and is a graduate of the University of California at Berkeley. He lives now in New York.